SYBIL LUDINGTON

Freedom's Brave Rider

Sybil heard the rooster crow in the barnyard. She slowly opened her eyes. Through the window, she saw a cloudless sky.

"It's going to be a beautiful day," she said to herself. "I hope Mother will let me go for a ride this afternoon."

Quietly, Sybil rolled out of bed. The wood floors were cold beneath her bare feet. She dressed quickly and went downstairs. Her mother was already busy fixing breakfast.

"Good morning, Sybil. I'm glad that you're up. There is much to be done today. I can use an extra pair of hands to knead this dough. I want to bake bread this morning."

"There's always much to be done, Mother. If I finish my chores, may I go for a ride this afternoon? The weather is good, and I think Star could use the exercise."

"We'll see," her mother answered. "Right now, get busy with that dough."

Sybil rolled up her sleeves and got to work. With eight children and a farm to run, there was always plenty to be done.

Sybil Ludington lived more than two hundred years ago on a farm in New York. Life was different back then. People couldn't just buy what they needed. Instead of going to the grocery store, they had to grow food at home. In the spring and summer, Sybil helped plant and weed the garden. In the fall, she helped harvest and can the fruits and vegetables. They had to put up enough food in the summer and fall to last all winter and spring.

Instead of buying clothes, they had to make their clothes by hand. Sybil helped with the sewing and mending. She also knew how to spin, weave, and knit. She helped with the washing and the making of soap, too. Making soap was her least favorite job. She always groaned when her mother announced, "Sybil, we need to make soap today."

In addition to daily farm chores, there were always her sisters and brothers to watch. Sybil was glad her sister Rebecca, just two years younger, was old enough to help with all of these jobs.

"You've put in a good day's work," Sybil's mother called to her later that day. "Now you can go for a ride like you wanted. Be careful, though. Remember, there could be enemy soldiers around. Stay out of the woods, too. Outlaws have been spotted close by."

"I'll be careful, Mother. I promise," Sybil said as she grabbed her coat. In just a few minutes, she was saddling the family horse. His name was Star because he had a white patch shaped like a star in the middle of his forehead. Sybil was a good rider and had been training the young horse for a year.

Sybil led Star out the barn door, put her foot into the stirrup, and jumped onto his back. Soon, she was galloping through the nearby fields. The wind felt good in her face. The birds were singing, the wildflowers were blooming, and the air was fresh. Sybil loved to ride. She felt as free as the wind itself.

Sybil remembered her mother's warnings and slowed down. Things had changed in the last few years. There was a difference in the country. Some people were unhappy about being ruled by Britain and King George. They wanted to be free to make their own laws. Other people wanted to stay under British rule. They were called Tories.

Sybil's father was on the side of those who wanted freedom for the colonies. On July 4, 1776, the Declaration of Independence had been signed. Three days later, New York voted for independence and became a free state instead of a British colony. The twelve other colonies voted for independence, too. These thirteen colonies became the United States of America. General George Washington became head of the American army fighting for freedom.

Sybil's father was a colonel in the army. He headed a militia of over 400 men. He also had spies reporting to him about British plans. Enoch Crosby was an important spy who sometimes came to the Ludington house. There were secret places in the house where a spy could hide.

Sybil helped the spies when her father was away from home. She learned her father's signal code. Then, Sybil could guide Enoch and other spies to safety.

One day, Sybil's father handed her a note. He asked, "Sybil, can you take Star and give this note to Enoch? He's hiding in the woods near the blueberry patch. I don't think anyone will suspect a young girl as a messenger."

"I can do it, Father. I want to help win our freedom."

"Be careful, Sybil. This message is very important. It has to get to Enoch. It can't fall into enemy hands. Do you understand?"

"Yes, I understand. I'll be careful. I'll make sure Enoch gets it."

Sybil hid the note in her shoe and rode down the lane on Star. She didn't see anybody following her. When Sybil got near the blueberry patch, she slowed down. Suddenly, Enoch jumped out of the bushes.

"Quick, Sybil, give me the note from your father," he whispered. Enoch looked nervous.

Sybil took the note out of her shoe and handed it to him.

"Thank you, Sybil. Good work. Now, get home safely," Enoch said as he dove back into the bushes. He disappeared just as quickly as he had come.

Sybil wondered what was in the note, but she had not read it. Could it mean the difference between winning and losing a battle? She turned Star toward home. She was happy that she had delivered the message safely.

Colonel Ludington's life was always in danger. The British offered a large reward for his capture. One night, troops loyal to Britain surrounded the Ludingtons' farmhouse. Sybil and Rebecca were on the lookout from the upstairs windows.

Suddenly, Sybil saw something move. "Look over there at the edge of the woods!" she cried.

Rebecca looked where Sybil was pointing. "Someone is out there! Over there, too," she said, pointing in another direction.

Sybil thought for only a moment. Then she said, "Quick, let's light candles in all the windows. Get Mother and the other children. Tell them to walk around in front of the windows. We'll make the soldiers think we have many people here. They won't dare attack, but I'll get our muskets ready, just in case."

The family did as Sybil asked. It worked! Soon the raiding party left. The danger had passed. Sybil's family was safe.

Sybil's biggest test of courage came on an April night in 1777. It was less than a month after her sixteenth birthday. Colonel Ludington had just returned home. He had been gone for many weeks with his militia, gathering supplies for the army. No British troops, called Redcoats, were in the area. General Washington was a two-day march away with his army. He said that Colonel Ludington's men could go home for spring planting.

That night, the Ludington family had a good dinner. Then, they settled down in front of the fire. The fire felt good because the weather had turned nasty. It was raining hard outside, and a cold wind was blowing. Sybil was glad to have her father home. He was glad to be home, too.

Suddenly, there was a loud knock on the front door. Colonel Ludington was alarmed. He rose and went to the door. Sybil followed her father and stood behind him.

"Who's there?" he shouted. "Identify yourself!"

It was a young man from Danbury, Connecticut. Colonel Ludington knew him and opened the door. The young man fell into the room. He was sopping wet and exhausted.

"Help!" he cried. "Danbury needs help. The Redcoats have come in from the sea. They're looting the town," he gasped, pausing for breath. "They've found the storehouse of army supplies," he continued. "They're taking what they want and burning the rest."

Danbury was just over the state border, a half-day's march from the Ludingtons' farm. Colonel Ludington knew General Washington's army was too far away to help Danbury and save the supplies. The colonel needed to gather his men together quickly. If he could, they might be able to get to Danbury in time to stop the British. How could he get word to his men? He turned to the young man from Danbury.

"Do you think you could ride through the countryside and deliver a message to my men?" Colonel Ludington asked.

"I don't know, sir, but I'll try," the messenger said.

Sybil interrupted. "He's too tired, Father. Also, he doesn't know which houses to go to. He would surely get captured."

"That may be true, Sybil, but I can't go. I have to stay here to organize my troops," her father replied.

"I can go, Father. I know the countryside, and I know the right houses."

"Oh, no!" Sybil's mother protested. "It's much too dangerous! Can't someone else go?"

"Mother, there is no one else!" Sybil said. "Think of the poor people of Danbury. Think of all those supplies that the army needs."

"Sybil's right," her father said. "She's the only one who can do it."

Mrs. Ludington turned to her daughter. "There is a difference between riding on a nice, sunny day and riding on a dark, stormy night. Are you sure you can do this?" she asked.

"I have to, Mother," Sybil replied. "It's too important not to try."

"Sybil, you must hurry," her father said. "There is no time to lose. But be careful. Don't let any Tories hear you. Watch out for outlaws in the woods, too. They are even more dangerous."

Mrs. Ludington brought Sybil their warmest cloak. She tucked some bread and beef jerky into Sybil's pocket. Then, she hugged her daughter tightly.

Colonel Ludington went out to the barn with Sybil. He helped her saddle Star. After Sybil climbed into the saddle, the colonel handed her a big stick.

"Beat on the front doors with this," he said. "It will save time because you won't have to dismount." Then, he wished his daughter luck and watched as she rode away into the night.

Sybil's mother was right. It was much different riding at night. The rain beat down on her. In minutes, Sybil was soaked. Her cloak and clothes were wet and heavy.

There were no moon or stars to guide her. The storm clouds blotted them out. Star was a good horse, though. He skillfully followed the road to the first farmhouse. Sybil rode right up to the front door. She raised her stick and beat on the door.

"Who's there?" the farmer shouted from inside.

"Sybil Ludington, the colonel's daughter. The militia is needed! Gather at the farm!" Sybil shouted. Then, she turned and headed for the next house.

The first farms were the easiest. They were closest to her home, so she knew the way. Sybil had ridden to them many times before. But soon the ride became more difficult. She had to slow down to make sure she didn't lose her way. It was pitch black, and the rain blew in her face, making it hard to see. Even the trees looked different at night. Their branches looked like arms reaching out to grab her. Sybil thought of everyone at home in front of the fire. She started wishing she was back there with them. Then, she shook her head.

"Thinking like that won't help," she said out loud. Star whinnied. That made her laugh.

"Are you agreeing with me, Star?" she asked as she patted his neck. "You're a good friend, Star. We'll get through this together."

Sybil felt better talking to Star. She had never been out by herself at night before. It was scarier than she had realized it would be. She just kept thinking about the poor people of Danbury. That kept her going.

The rain was making the ground very muddy. The footing was slippery as they went around Lake Mahopac, but Star and Sybil pressed on. Farmer after farmer was awakened by loud knocking. Each of them was surprised to see a girl on horseback out on such a terrible night. Several of them tried to persuade her to take a rest inside. Their wives offered her tea and something to eat. Sybil wished she could accept the kind offers, but she knew that she couldn't. She had to complete her mission as fast as she could.

The young girl and her horse continued riding through the countryside. After several miles, Sybil spotted the dark shapes of several houses ahead.

"Slow down, Star," she said, patting the horse's neck. "We're nearing a town. We'll have to be quiet. We don't want to alert the wrong people."

Star shook his head. Sybil pulled on the reins, bringing him to a walk. Suddenly, a dog started barking as they passed the first house. He ran out and nipped at Star's hooves. Sybil bent over Star's neck and patted his side.

"Steady, boy," she said softly as she urged Star forward. The dog kept barking at them. Sybil kept an eye on the dark house. She saw someone light a candle and open an upstairs window.

A man shouted, "Who goes there?"

Sybil knew this house belonged to a Tory. She
stayed bent over Star, hoping the man couldn't see
her. A gust of wind blew the rain down even harder.
But the wind and rain weren't all bad. They blew the
Tory's candle out. He slammed the window shut. He
hadn't seen them.

After a minute, Sybil and Star had passed the
house. The dog stopped barking, turned, and went
home. Sybil patted Star's neck again. "Good boy,"
she said. "You did just fine. I guess that old dog didn't
want to get as cold and wet as we are."

Next, Sybil headed for the blacksmith's shop. She'd been there before with her father. She knew where it was, and she knew he was a militiaman. When Sybil got there, she slid off Star's back. She didn't dare knock loudly with the stick. She might wake up neighbors who were Tories.

Sybil had to knock several times, but finally the front door opened. The blacksmith held up a lantern to see who was there.

"Why, is that you, Sybil Ludington? What are you doing out on a night like this?" he asked.

"The British are looting Danbury! The militia is needed," she told him. "I'm spreading the word."

"I'll get my musket. Then I'll make sure all our militiamen in town know that they're needed. We'll head for your father's farm."

"Thank you," she said, as she climbed back into her saddle. "That will save me some valuable time."

Sybil left town and quickly found her path going through the woods. She felt more alone and scared than ever. This was perfect outlaw country. She held tightly onto her big stick. She might have to use it to keep the outlaws away.

"Keep your ears open, Star," Sybil whispered. "If outlaws see us, we'll have to make a run for it. We can't let them catch us."

Suddenly, Star stopped. He shook his head. Sybil urged him forward, but he didn't move.

"What is it, Star?" Sybil whispered.

Sybil sat very still. Then, she noticed the smell of smoke in the air.

"A campfire!" she whispered. "Only outlaws would be camping on a night like this! Thanks for the warning, Star."

Sybil quietly dismounted. She took the reins and went in front of Star. She walked slowly, leading the horse. They hardly made a sound. The rain helped muffle their footsteps.

Then, Sybil spotted the light from a campfire through the trees. She could see four men sitting in a circle around it.

Sybil stopped, frozen with fear. The outlaws would love to get their hands on a good horse like Star. What would they do to her? Would she ever see her family again? Sybil clenched her fists. She couldn't think about that now. They had to complete their mission.

Sybil took one step, then another. Each step was a victory over her fear. She was almost past them, when suddenly one of the outlaw's horses whinnied. He must have sensed that Star was near. Sybil was startled. She felt like she had jumped a mile. Star skittered, but she held him tight.

"Who's out there?" one of the outlaws yelled.

"Probably just some critter," another outlaw answered. "It's too miserable a night for anyone to be out riding."

"Well, go make sure," the first one ordered. "Take a good look around. I don't want anyone sneaking up on us."

That was enough for Sybil. She jumped on Star's back and dug her heel into his side.

"Run, Star, run! Don't let them catch us!" she told him urgently.

Star took off. He galloped over the slippery path. They raced through the woods. Rain stung Sybil's face. Then, low-hanging branches whipped into her. One caught her cape. She heard it rip. Another hit her in the face. She knew she must be bleeding, but she didn't care. She just wanted to get away from the outlaws.

Finally, Star and Sybil came out of the woods. As Star slowed down, Sybil looked back. No one was following them.

"Good, Star," she said, while they both caught their breath. "Good."

Sybil remembered the bread and beef jerky that her mother had given her. She reached into her pocket. The bread was a wet, soggy mess, but the beef jerky would do. She was too hungry to care that it was all wet, too.

"A cup of hot tea would really taste good with this jerky, Star," she said. "I'm sorry I don't have anything for you. When we get home, I'll make sure you get some nice, dry oats. I'll get you an apple from the root cellar, too. You deserve a special treat."

The weather improved a bit as Sybil and Star rode on. The wind became less gusty, and the rain lessened. Sybil made good time as she went from farmhouse to farmhouse, waking militiamen. She safely made it through several small towns. Each time, she found the right households to alert.

Then, Sybil found herself in a rocky area. It was even worse than the mud had been. It was difficult for Star to get his footing. Sybil was afraid he'd injure himself. She jumped down and tried to pick the safest path through the rocks. Her feet were numb with cold. She could hardly feel her fingers holding Star's reins.

Looking up, Sybil saw a glow in the distance. Could it be sunrise already? No, she thought, it's still too early for dawn. Then, it came to her. It was Danbury. The British were burning the town!

"Oh, Star," she cried. "Look at what the Redcoats are doing! Will our militia be able to stop them? We've got to get to the last houses so Father can get started. The British must be turned back!"

Sybil once again mounted Star. She was more determined than ever to finish her mission. They picked their way through the rocks and were once again galloping toward militiamen's homes.

Uphill and downhill she went, banging on doors until she could hardly lift her stick. She shouted her warning until she was hoarse. She was cold, wet, and exhausted, but Sybil would not give up.

Finally, the last house had been alerted. Sybil could head for home.

"Star, we did it!" she cried. "We really did it."

Sybil thought of how wonderful it would be to see her own home again. She dreamed of changing into warm clothes and sitting in front of a roaring fire with a hot meal and a cup of tea.

She patted Star's neck. "I won't forget your bag of oats or your apple," she told him.

Then, she looked up with a jerk. Was that horses she heard up ahead? Could it be outlaws—or even Redcoats?

No! It was some of the very militiamen she had alerted. They were heading for her home, too. She and Star were safe!

When they reached the farm, Sybil saw the field full of men. Her father was readying them for the march to Danbury. The men sent up a cheer when they saw her. Colonel Ludington turned. He ran to Sybil's side and helped her down.

"You did it, Sybil! Good work, girl!" he cried as he gave her a big hug.

Mrs. Ludington came running out of the house. She pulled Sybil close, crying, "You're safe! You made it home safely!"

Then all of her sisters and brothers came running out of the house, too. "Sybil's home!" they shouted as they gathered around her.

Sybil was taken into the house. Soon she was in warm clothes, sitting in front of a roaring fire with a hot meal. She made sure Star was taken care of, too.

Colonel Ludington and his militia headed for Danbury. The town was burned, but the militia chased the British all the way back to the sea. No other towns were harmed. The militiamen recaptured many of the supplies that had been stolen by the Redcoats. Colonel Ludington and his militia had turned a victory for the British into a defeat.

Sybil Ludington was a hero. She had ridden over 40 miles in almost nine hours. General Washington came to the farm to meet her. She inspired many people during those difficult years of the American Revolution. Many years later, a statue of Sybil and Star was built to honor their courage. It can be seen today on the shore of Lake Mahopac in Carmel, New York.

Statue of Sybil Ludington in Carmel, NY